AF450079

ATHEISM IS NOT A RELIGION

Eduard Honey

ATHEISM IS NOT A RELIGION

Religions Are a Human Invention

EDITORIAL
LETRA MINÚSCULA

First edition: September 2023
ISBN: 978-84-19978-84-4
Copyright © 2023 Eduard Honey
Edited by Editorial Letra Minúscula
www.letraminuscula.com
contacto@letraminuscula.com

CONTENTS

ATHEISM IS FREEDOM

Atheism is NOT a religion! No matter how often this lie is repeated, it doesn't become less false. In this book, we'll debunk this myth and many other misconceptions about atheists.

Why do some people think atheism is a religion? The answer can help us understand many of the false accusations that theists regularly make against atheism.

This happens because they operate within a theological frame of thought, which they also use to judge atheists. They believe that if someone criticizes religion, they wish to replace it with another different religion, or if God is rejected, it's because we want to replace Him with another deity.

In this regard, we need to understand the misguided words of Pope Benedict XVI during his visit to Spain for the 2011 World Youth Day. Referring to atheists and agnostics, he stated that "many, considering themselves gods, think they have no need for roots or foundations other than themselves." He thus associated atheism with the supposed attempt to turn humans into God.

The mistake theists make here is to theologically judge something that is opposed to that kind of thinking and doesn't belong to that conceptual framework. That's why they're unable to interpret atheism as the denial of the existence of God or any kind of deity. Atheism, contrary to what some say, is neither a religion nor a faith, nor does it aspire to replace God with something else.

Atheism would be dogmatic if atheists were not willing to change their initial position of denying God and other deities when presented with undeniable evidence to the contrary—a case we believe theism has yet to make.

Atheism is freedom of thought. It's about not following authorities but only facts. It's about upholding a moderate skepticism that makes us question everything. It's about not accepting anything as true unless there's evidence to support it.

WHAT IS A RELIGION?

Defining what constitutes a religion is undoubtedly not an easy task. The challenge lies in the multitude of vastly different religious expressions, making it nearly impossible to craft a definition that encompasses all without being overly vague and ambiguous—qualities that should never be associated with an operational definition.

The etymology of the term "religion" might help us in this endeavor. Traditionally, two meanings have been linked to this word. One of them, derived from a passage by Cicero (*De natura deorum*, in English, *On the Nature of the Gods*), connects "religion" to the word *religens*, the opposite of *negligens* (negligent). In this sense, a "religious" person (*religiosi*) would be prudent and meticulous, performing tasks with care and attention. This would point toward a moral quality of the person.

The second etymological origin proposed associates "religion" with *religare*, meaning to bind or tie. Religion indicates a connection with the divine. A religious person would be linked to God.

Both origins are important because they unveil two fundamental dimensions of the concept: the moral and the transcendent.

Every religion develops, to varying extents, a moral code, basic ideas about what's right and wrong. The complexity depends on the conceptual development of the religion in question. We have religions like Christianity or Islam that possess comprehensive moral codes that pertain to nearly every facet of our lives, both public and private. There might be other religions less advanced in this aspect, where the moral aspect is limited to general principles like "respect the elderly" or similar formulations.

However, the presence of a collective morality is not a sufficient criterion to define a religion. There must be a supernatural reality, a God, or gods from whom these ethical principles emanate, conveyed to people through prophets, shamans, or others believed to interpret divine will.

In other words, we're discussing religion when one or several entities (which we can label as "God" or many other names) exist beyond our known natural world, typically endowed with powers far exceeding ours.

This supernatural aspect, in isolation, isn't enough to define a religion. Ghosts, for instance, are supernatural entities but are unrelated to gods. One can believe in spirits while rejecting religion. Religions are based on belief in a supernatural reality, but not all such beliefs are religions. This distinction seems clear to me.

In the previous paragraph, I mentioned "collective morality." This phrase wasn't chosen lightly. I contend that another defining characteristic of a religion is the presence of a community of believers. A set of beliefs based on some deity conceived and followed by a single individual can hardly be labeled a religion. To discuss religion, even a very small group of followers for that belief system is necessary.

Another central point is that religions are grounded in beliefs that cannot be rationally proven. A religion is not a scientific theory. This is why its core beliefs rely on faith, even if these beliefs contradict our understanding of nature's laws—a point of little concern to religious followers since they believe in a supernatural reality that doesn't abide by our known natural laws.

A feature that also characterizes religion is the presence of charismatic leaders, prophets, shamans, or others who have a direct, or closer, communion with the divine. Hence, many religions have hierarchical structures where the leaders bridge the believers' relationship with their respective deities.

These leaders could be living individuals or ancient prophets through whom God relayed His revealed word and the precepts the faithful should adhere to. Sometimes, this spiritual leader might act as a ritual teacher, a transmitter of spirits' or God's messages. This figure is charismatic, an authority guiding others in their rapport with the supernatural.

Lastly, I'd like to emphasize a feature that seems common to the majority of religions: the performance of ritualistic acts aimed at venerating the divine. These might range from elaborate symbolic ceremonies like the Catholic Mass to tribal dances and chants intended to earn the gods' favor for a bountiful harvest. Ritual and symbolism play pivotal roles in religions.

ATHEISM IS NOT A RELIGION

One of the criticisms that believers often level against atheists is the following: atheism is a religion. Pope John Paul II, in his encyclical *Fides et ratio*, also denounced "various forms of atheistic humanism, philosophically constructed, which portrayed faith as harmful and alienating to the full development of rationality." These forms of humanism, he claimed, "did not hesitate to present themselves as new religions."

In my opinion, there are six characteristics that define a religion:

1. A collective morality based on divinity.
2. Belief in a supernatural reality.
3. The existence of a community of believers.
4. A core set of beliefs founded on faith.
5. The presence of individuals who guide followers in their relationship with the divine.
6. The practice of rituals dedicated to divine worship.

What I'm going to do next is determine if atheism meets any or all of these characteristics.

Clearly, the first one doesn't apply. An atheist cannot subscribe to a morality grounded in God simply because they don't believe in Him. This doesn't mean, as many believers suggest, that an atheist doesn't believe in objective morality. An atheist might or might not, but they reject the idea that moral foundations are based on a deity.

Being an atheist doesn't necessarily make one a relativist or nihilist who believes there's no difference between right and wrong. Being an atheist doesn't mean one is wicked, hedonistic, or selfish, focused solely on personal pleasure or welfare. There's no inherent link between belief in God and morally correct behavior.

The second characteristic isn't as straightforward. While an atheist denies the existence of a supernatural reality like God, gods, or other deities, they might believe in supernatural entities like ghosts.

Though theoretically possible, this isn't common. I'd argue that most atheists extend their denial of God and religion to everything we might label as supernatural. So, we must dismiss this second characteristic, with the nuances I've highlighted.

The third characteristic: the existence of a community of believers. Indeed, atheist associations and groups exist worldwide. The widespread acceptance of atheism in our era is a historical novelty. It wasn't until the 20th century, primarily due to communism, that atheism became a widespread movement aiming for dominance.

Because of religion's historical dominance, atheists were often isolated individuals, hiding their beliefs out of fear of persecution, imprisonment, or execution. But atheist associations seem no different from sports clubs, gourmet societies, scientific bodies, or any other community formed around shared interests. And they seem fundamentally different from religions.

This is because atheists don't worship anything and don't consider themselves united by common faith, even if they share similar worldviews. So, atheism doesn't seem to meet this religious characteristic.

The fourth trait mentions a "core set of beliefs founded on faith." An atheist notes the lack of objective proof for theism. This stance arises from reason, not faith or irrational belief.

Any reasonable atheist would reconsider their atheism if presented with solid evidence or rationale. You can't debate the core beliefs of a religious follower because they're beyond any logical argument. Therefore, atheism doesn't meet this criterion either.

The fifth and sixth characteristics can be addressed together with a negative response. Within atheism, there can't be religious leaders (like the Pope, a shaman, or a rabbi) guiding the faithful in their relationship with a deity, simply because atheists deny any form of God.

In atheistic literature, there might be influential authors like Nietzsche or Marx. But these figures don't equate to spiritual guides. There can be leading thinkers, just as there are in biology, mathematics, or spelunking, but they don't compare to the prophets of world religions.

Also, I'm unaware of any atheism-related ritual practiced by its adherents. Someone might argue that civil marriages or secular child-welcoming ceremonies, which might replace Christian baptisms, are atheistic acts. Yet, these ceremonies don't celebrate atheism, even if participants are atheists. Many get married in the Catholic Church without believing its tenets because they find the ceremony more appealing or wish to maintain a family tradition. Participating in these secular acts doesn't imply any connection with atheism; deeply religious individuals might have a civil marriage because they're divorced and haven't annulled their previous church wedding.

The conclusion from this brief analysis is clear: atheism is not a religion.

THE FALSE SADNESS OF THE ATHEIST

Not believing in God, or in any supernatural entity, doesn't push us toward melancholy or suicide. Quite the opposite. I believe that it should be an incentive to value life as a phenomenal occurrence in the universe, the result of millions of chance events that led us to this moment.

If nothing exists after death, we can't grieve or await a better future that will never come. This realization should drive us to strive for a better world, one where the maximum number of humans can pursue their life goals and achieve happiness.

For centuries, humanity waited for life to pass by, hoping for the hereafter. It disregarded pain, considering it a divine punishment for our sins. This makes theism a hurdle in the battle against evil, despite what its defenders might argue.

Ever since a significant portion of humanity freed itself from the mental shackles of religion, we've increasingly taken charge of our destiny. Hence, we must work toward minimizing suffering and building just and free societies. Atheism might be the best way to appreciate the surrounding beauty and work to ensure reason's light overpowers the shadows of ignorance and fear.

RELIGION AND EMPATHY

Empathy is the ability to step into another's shoes. It's understanding that what others experience and feel mirrors our own emotions. Its biggest enemy is selfishness—the false belief that we are isolated islands interacting solely for personal gain. This is untrue, for we are fundamentally interconnected, even if we remain unaware of it.

Numerous barriers hinder empathy, and religion stands as a prime obstacle. For millennia, religious leaders have promised universal love and harmony among humans. Yet, what we've received is fanaticism, wars, and violence. The paradise pledged by almost all religions has morphed into hell. Most people follow a religious belief, yet our world is submerged in conflict and torn by pain.

Why is this? The answer is straightforward. We've built an ideal more significant than the very individuals it concerns, making empathy impossible. Religion binds us to doctrines and blind obedience to ecclesiastical hierarchies, self-declared custodians of these dogmatic beliefs. Life becomes secondary to the divine revelations defended by major religions.

We can never put ourselves in another's shoes if we believe they are insignificant compared to the absolute truth of religion. And there can be no empathy when we are not truly free to understand others and ourselves. Faith is not a form of freedom, but an accepted bondage. If someone chooses to be a slave, they are not free; they remain a prisoner, even if it is by their own volition.

For empathy to blossom, we must relinquish dogma and refrain from constructing absolutes that eventually become tools for societal control. Only by foregoing the security of following others can we find the path to truth. When divisive ideals vanish, empathy naturally ensues. If only we realized that what binds us is more potent than what divides, ceaseless conflicts and battles would become pointless.

IMPERFECT JUSTICE

Christianity tries to explain evil by resorting to the concept of original sin. God creates humans, Adam and Eve, and settles them in Eden, where they enjoy a paradisiacal existence. But Satan tempts Eve, convincing her to eat the forbidden fruit from the tree of knowledge. She persuades Adam to taste it, leading God to banish them from Paradise. Upon expulsion, God tells Adam, "Cursed is the ground because of you; through painful toil you will eat food from it all the days of your life" (Genesis 3:17). The disobedience of the first man and woman condemns humanity to a tarnished world ridden with evil.

This predicament can only be rectified during the Final Judgment, when our world will vanish and be purified, creating "a new heaven and a new earth" (Revelation 21:1), where God will "wipe away every tear" and death and pain will be no more (21:4). However, only the righteous will enjoy God's presence in this new Eden. The wicked will suffer eternally in the "lake of burning sulfur" (21:8).

Thus, evil can coexist with a benevolent God. The infant gassed in Auschwitz will be resurrected, living eternally with loved ones if deemed worthy. Their murderers, in contrast, will endure endless torment in the fiery lake. In this manner, God's infallible justice triumphs, and the righteous are rewarded.

From my atheistic standpoint, this narrative defies reason. It's a mythological creation with perhaps literary appeal, but it fails to solve the crux of the issue. Atheists believe evil doesn't require myths about Eden or bizarre lakes of fire as explanations.

The perfect justice attained post-Final Judgment merely reflects an unattainable wish. No verdict can compensate parents mourning a murdered child. But a hypothetical God could, possessing the power to resurrect and judge souls.

Regrettably, such impeccable justice is beyond human reach, merely an unreachable fantasy. All we can do is strive to improve our flawed justice system.

SPIRITUAL EXPERIENCES

In his book *Atheism in Our Time* (1967, p. 287), Giacomo Soleri asserts that there is one aspect underlying all forms of atheism, which he terms "the phenomenic autonomy of immediate experience." What does this mean? He is referring to "the autonomy of the natural order, understandable in its being and in its operation without needing to resort to divinity to justify it." That is to say, nature suffices in itself and can find an explanation for its operation and its very existence without invoking God.

The denial of the existence of God, for Giacomo Soleri, is grounded in the fact that scientists and philosophers exclude "from the plane of existence everything that cannot be verified by the senses or their work tools." Only what can be the subject of scientific experimentation would exist for them, excluding the existence of God. This author also makes a statement that many other theists do not share: "We will never find traces of God in our investigation of the world."

However, this does not necessarily lead to atheism because: "There are truths that are neither tangible nor scientifically verifiable because they belong to a higher, metaphysical plane that regulates 'from within' the lives of beings, things, and men. Among this interweaving of spiritual experiences that fill human life and are untranslatable into scientific experiences—love, goodness, beauty, truth...—is included the existence of God."

This author is right when he claims that atheists don't need to invoke God to explain the world. But to defend his theism, he posits the existence of a "higher plane" of spiritual experiences that includes religious experience. In doing so, Soleri conflates different matters.

All atheists can experience love or beauty, like anyone else, without invoking a higher reality. However, the experience of something is not proof of the existence of what provokes the experience. Theists are not satisfied with speaking of a divine experience; they claim that the God they experience genuinely exists beyond that experience.

The beauty we feel when looking at a painting doesn't need an ideal notion of beauty that exists in some metaphysical reality, as Plato believed. Thus, it's a mistake to compare these ideas with the existence of God.

After thousands of years of various theistic spiritual experiences, we still lack a single objective proof of the existence of the gods or deities that supposedly induce them.

WHY I'M NOT AGNOSTIC

In his renowned *Dictionary of Philosophy*, José Ferrater Mora states that "an agnostic does not declare, for instance, that God doesn't exist, but that they don't know whether God exists or not." He also mentions that "E. Tierno Galván has distinguished between atheism and agnosticism, highlighting that while in the former there's a will for God not to exist, in the latter there isn't."

I find this claim by Tierno Galván to be misguided. It's one of the many falsehoods said about atheism. Atheism isn't about wishing for God's nonexistence; it's a rational hypothesis based on our current understanding of the world. And all indications suggest that the omnipotent being many religions believe in is a myth.

Agnostics claim that the nonexistence of God (or the supernatural) hasn't been proven, and therefore, we can't comment on the matter. Here's something I keep repeating: the burden of proof lies with the one making the claim. And after thousands of years of theistic beliefs, their followers have not provided a single objective proof of the existence of supernatural beings.

Agnosticism forgets that there's a pre-existing knowledge of the world provided to us by science. And everything we know about nature contradicts the existence of supernatural beings or gods. Someone rising from the dead or walking on water goes against all the laws of physics and biology that we know.

Atheism isn't a dogma or the expression of a personal desire; it's a probabilistic rational hypothesis that can be refuted if new evidence arises. If tomorrow it were proven beyond any reasonable doubt that a God exists, atheists should reconsider their stance.

Unfortunately for theists, this has not happened, nor does it seem likely to in the future. All our scientific knowledge leads us to believe that the God many worship is just a product of our imagination.

I believe I'm not mistaken when I say that often agnosticism is the mask under which some unconfessed theists hide, choosing the realm of "not knowing" to maintain irrational beliefs. Agnostics, perhaps unintentionally in many cases, end up being the perfect allies of theists, giving them free rein for their ideas.

CRITIQUE OF ATHEISM

In his book *Lessons on Contemporary Atheism* (Gredos, 1971), Roger Verneaux critiques atheism from theistic perspectives, specifically targeting Marxist and existentialist atheism. He believed these to be the only doctrinal forms of atheism worth studying, which was likely a reflection of the era in which he wrote this essay.

The atheism I advocate cannot be equated to either of these doctrines; I would label it as rationalist.

Verneaux posits that, for Marxism, the world is "self-explanatory: it contains all rationality and doesn't require any other explanation" (p. 29). Existentialism, on the other hand, sees the world as "anti-explanatory: it's absurd and resistant to any form of explanation."

In my view, the world can and should be explained through rationality and science by uncovering the laws of nature and rigorously reflecting on various human realities. This explanation should be immanent, meaning it should rely on the world itself and not on realities beyond human comprehension.

Yet, Verneaux believes that in both cases, the result is the same: metaphysics is discarded because humanity only opens itself to its own world and closes itself off to anything beyond.

The atheism I defend is fully compatible with metaphysics, as long as it's seen as a reflection on non-empirical concepts. But this metaphysics does not accept the existence of a supernatural "beyond" that can only be grasped by select individuals allegedly enlightened by God.

The issue arises when many theists equate metaphysics with their own theism (just as they equate God with goodness), leading them to mistakenly believe that rejecting theism equates to rejecting all of metaphysics.

According to Verneaux, this denial of metaphysics has a significant consequence: all paths to God, save faith, are shut off. This includes philosophical or rational avenues. In my view, the rational path is closed not because of the rejection of metaphysics (which would be suicidal for reason itself), but because it's currently impossible to rationally prove the existence of God given the evidence we have.

In the end, the only refuge left for the believer is their faith, choosing to ignore reality in favor of saying, "I believe." Reason has always played a secondary role within theism, as its foundation is the irrational belief in a supernatural realm.

REPLY TO PETER HIGGS

Peter Higgs made headlines worldwide due to the discovery of the boson named after him. This particle has been nick-named "the God particle." A moniker that has nothing to do with physics but is more about crafting an attention-grabbing headline.

When someone becomes an authority in a field, they are often asked about everything, even topics unrelated to their area of expertise.

A notable example of this is Albert Einstein, who is frequently quoted on almost any matter. I'm convinced that many quotes attributed to him are either not his or are taken out of context. Furthermore, Einstein's stance on religious matters was ambiguous. In some instances, he seemed theistic or pantheistic, while in others, atheistic. For instance, a recently auctioned letter from him stated, "The word God is for me nothing but an expression and product of human weakness, and the Bible is a collection of honorable but still primitive legends."

Regrettably, Peter Higgs has joined the ranks of scientists who offer opinions on both the mundane and the divine, with statements suggesting that science and religion "can coexist, as long as one is not dogmatic." Most religions uphold beliefs, like resurrection, that contradict centuries of scientific findings and dedicated research.

Science and religion are incompatible because the former relies on reason, a scientific method based on empirical data, and theories that can be disproven. Religion, on the other hand, clings to beliefs that cannot be objectively validated.

It's true that renowned scientists can be believers. Such contradictions exist in many individuals. In their labs, they apply a research method that would invalidate these religious beliefs, but then engage in worship of a deity for which they have no scientific evidence.

I also find his criticisms of Richard Dawkins regrettable: "I'm not against religious people unless they act like extreme fanatics. Dawkins' issue is that he targets fundamentalists, but obviously, not all believers are such. In that sense, sometimes it seems Dawkins himself adopts a fundamentalist stance, just at the opposite end."

I'd tell Mr. Higgs that I'm also not against religious individuals, and I don't believe Dawkins is either. The main concern is the veracity or falsity of religious beliefs and the implications of such ideologies. Most of us reject fanaticism, but that doesn't mean that more moderate believers are right. Battling fundamentalism with reason is not falling into what is criticized but rather a valuable contribution to the advancement of humanity.

RESPONSE TO BENEDICT XVI

Benedict XVI claims that the three paths to address atheism, skepticism, and religious indifference are: 1) the beauty of creation, 2) the discovery of an aspiration to infinity that every human being carries within, and 3) the testimony of faith born from an encounter with Christ.

This beauty argument isn't new. Believing that everything exists for our aesthetic pleasure seems like a senseless intellectual arrogance. It's striking to think that an omnipotent God created the universe, billions of galaxies, each containing billions of suns, and the purpose of this evolution, which took over 13.7 billion years, is our enjoyment. Why wait all this time for humans to emerge on a tiny planet? If this is the behavior of an omnipotent being, it doesn't reflect much intelligence, as humans could have been created from the start.

It's true that humans have an aspiration to infinity or, more precisely, a desire to transcend their limited existence. But this proves nothing. Wishing for immortality doesn't mean we are or that some intelligent being is. The gap between desire and reality is vast.

Regarding testimony, I'm reminded of a biblical passage that states, "It is easier for a camel to pass through the eye of a needle than for a rich man to enter the kingdom of God" (Matthew 19:24). It's contradictory for an elderly man surrounded by immense luxury and living in a palace to speak of testimony when the vast riches around him contradict Jesus' message.

What's lacking in the Catholic Church is a testimony of Christian life, especially among the ecclesiastical hierarchies that preach moral lessons to others.

FAITH IS IRRATIONAL

To deeply understand the religious phenomenon, we must address the analysis of the relationships between faith and reason. This involves delving into the essence of human beings and the connections between science and these kinds of beliefs. If we can grasp the psychological principles driving people to have faith, we will make substantial advancements in understanding ourselves.

Faith is belief in something without objective evidence supporting what we believe in. We must be cautious of the polysemous meaning this idea carries to prevent confusion with its different interpretations. Sometimes, the word "faith" is synonymous with trust. For example, many claim to have faith in the future or in a person, meaning they are confident things will turn out well or that they believe someone is trustworthy. This type of trust isn't necessarily negative, as it might be based on our rational judgment or our ability to assess someone's abilities. Here, I am not referring to that, but to faith in the religious context.

Faith is the acceptance of a truth that isn't rational. It's having a firm belief in something for which there is no evidence. If we had scientific confirmation of the existence of an omnipotent God (assuming this is even possible, as conceiving such a notion is undoubtedly challenging), religious faith wouldn't be necessary.

For those of us who don't believe in supernatural phenomena, if we were to witness the resurrection of the dead, the Final Judgment, and the manifestation of angels, devils, and all those fantastical beings spoken of in many religions, we'd undoubtedly be compelled to abandon our skepticism and accept these beliefs.

This brings us to one of the critical differences between faith and reason. Scientific propositions can be falsified, meaning it's hypothetically possible to present evidence proving a theory wrong. If there's no possibility of falsification, we are no longer in the realm of science but something else entirely.

Atheism, when rightly understood, is not an ideological dogmatism comparable to religions. True, there might be dogmatic atheists, and they've existed throughout history. However, those who fall into this error betray the genuine spirit of atheism, which should always arise from the freedom of reason, not from adherence to absurd ideological postulates.

Atheism is not a religion. It's a philosophical stance reached after rationally analyzing reality. It's a probabilistic hypothesis grounded in our current understanding of the world. There's always the chance that new evidence might make us abandon this atheistic hypothesis in the future. Undoubtedly, a scientific demonstration of God or religious truths should be incredibly clear. We must consider the remote possibility, no matter how unlikely, that we might be wrong, and that theism's truth might be proven someday. Honestly, I don't believe this will ever happen, though we should consider this theoretical hypothesis.

Many cling to their religious beliefs, seeking any seemingly rational loophole. They claim, incorrectly, that just as there's no evidence for divine existence, neither is there evidence against it. Faced with doubt, they prefer to keep believing, or they declare themselves agnostic when, deep down, they still harbor supernatural beliefs.

Those reasoning this way overlook an evident fact: the burden of proof lies with the claimant. One doesn't prove the nonexistence of something; those asserting that a God (or something similar) exists are the ones obliged to provide evidence for their beliefs.

Yet, after thousands of years of theistic beliefs, with brilliant minds in science and philosophy having constructed intricate arguments like the ontological one or Saint Thomas Aquinas' Five Ways, they haven't managed to produce a single objective proof supporting their faith's truth.

There's another fundamental element in this matter that's often overlooked. I'm referring to what I call prior knowledge. This term encompasses the collective scientific knowledge that humanity has accumulated throughout history. And everything we know about the universe and ourselves contradicts religious claims.

We can better understand this with an example. Most religions argue for the existence of a soul or an afterlife that begins after physical death. However, having studied the human body using increasingly sophisticated technology and with medicine making extraordinary progress over the last few centuries, we've never found any evidence of something we could call a soul—an immortal spirit that lives within us and leaves us at death.

Similarly, no one has ever returned from the dead, and I doubt that'll ever happen. Therefore, it's reasonable to think that these notions of a soul or immortal life are myths, though some might find this difficult to accept.

The most plausible assumption is that when someone dies, what we observe simply happens. Their body decomposes over time, and that person is gone forever. What remains of them are memories held by the living and their traces in this world, be it physical possessions or ideas recorded in some way.

All that we understand from nature—our scientific, medical, and physical knowledge—disproves theistic claims. Science contradicts religious assertions. I'm convinced that as we research more and understand this complex world, the realm of ignorance feeding faith will continue to shrink. Yet, it seems obvious that this won't impact believers much. They'll cling to their beliefs as they always have, unfazed by any scientific discovery that might refute them. Nothing from science will change their minds.

At its core, this entire topic of religion, which seems incredibly complex, is simple. World libraries are filled with countless books trying to prove divine existence, reflecting on religious texts, or considering the words of prophets, or even a supposed God who came to Earth to sacrifice for us. Incredibly intricate arguments try to justify true faith. We need to approach this topic from a more radical viewpoint, with a mind free from biases and uninfluenced by a tradition that holds us back.

If we can do that, we'll uncover a truth that seems clear to me. Humans crafted religion to address internal needs, answer their ignorance, fears, and deepest desires. They fear death. They don't want to die or be separated from loved ones. They're unsure about the universe's origins and can't answer their existence's fundamental questions. Thus, they come up with religion, soul, or reincarnation ideas.

Their reality doesn't satisfy them. They want to exist forever, hoping for a flawless justice system that rewards the good with eternal paradise while punishing the wicked. Unable to have all this, and viewing the world as bleak in many aspects, they develop intricate religious mythologies—answers to their deepest yearnings. It's not God creating humans, but humans inventing God to address their desires, ignorance, and the fears tightening their hearts.

Where science can't reach, the gap of ignorance can always be filled by religious faith. The happier the world, the lesser the need to believe in gods. Hence, there's a clear link between progress and atheism. The most advanced countries tend to have the highest number of atheists. In less developed regions, like Africa, atheism is virtually nonexistent.

Regardless of our cultural and economic advancements, there's always the pain of death and the desire to find life's transcendent meaning. That's why, regardless of our technical progress, religions will always have grounds to thrive.

Proof of a society achieving material development while retaining a strong religious foundation is evident in the United States. One of the most advanced societies, yet where religion remains central.

To combat religious phenomena, a mental shift is needed, a deep understanding of our intellect, and the reasons that lead us to embrace religious faith.

One of the significant missteps of many religions, particularly Christianity, is prompting the acceptance of evil in the world as a natural, inevitable outcome, resulting from the original sin which we are deemed responsible for. Christians sanctify suffering and worship a crucified God who came into this world to die for us.

What we should do instead is not glorify the suffering but fight relentlessly to end pain in the world.

Christianity posits that humans are to blame for all their suffering and that our inherent destiny is eternal suffering. It further claims that such profound pain can only be overcome through the intervention of a merciful God.

This viewpoint is deeply flawed. While we are indeed responsible for a significant portion of suffering since we could end many of the afflictions that plague humanity, some people still go hungry or live in abject poverty despite the level of progress achieved. This, undeniably, is one of the strongest indicators of human irrationality and selfishness. Moreover, there are "natural," evils, like disasters (earthquakes, cyclones, etc.) or diseases, for which we can't be blamed.

Discussing collective responsibility for evil often overshadows the individual responsibility each of us holds. We are accountable for our actions, as long as we are of sound mind, and must face the consequences. Glorifying and sanctifying suffering, constructing altars to exalt it, is misplaced; our true calling is to combat it.

Faith, to me, seems one of the gravest creations of the human mind. It epitomizes the extent of our irrationality. We wish to believe and accept a higher truth without tangible evidence, showcasing the victory of desire and emotion over reason.

Faith is a self-imposed intellectual prison that most of humanity is unwilling to escape. It's the act of accepting something merely because we desire it, refusing to see the obvious and betraying the critical spirit everyone should possess.

Theists often wrongly argue that everyone holds faith in something and that religious faith is no different from the convictions of atheists. They argue this way because they're confined within their religious framework, assuming we all share their worldview. Hence, they suggest atheism is a religion, or scientists have "faith" in their theories.

Such reasoning is flawed and unfounded. Atheism, at least the version I endorse, and science are based on rational judgment, not on blind adherence to so-called authorities. Their essence is, thus, fundamentally different.

Religious organizations employ faith to control their followers, shackling our minds. Many religious leaders claim a unique connection with the deity worshipped by their followers, presenting themselves as direct conduits of divine authority. They aren't pressed to justify their beliefs but merely instruct their followers to believe without questioning.

By placing faith in a person or a specific belief, we suspend critical thinking and the moderate skepticism that should permeate all aspects of our lives.

Regrettably, most either don't want the trouble of thinking independently or don't know how to. They'd rather others dictate truth and falsehood to them. This offers a sense of security, easy answers, and belonging when backed by a significant social group. Religion meets our internal needs and addresses our fear of death.

However, this comes at a cost: self-betrayal. We forsake our freedom, willingly entering the prison of faith guarded by the jailer of dogma. Dogmatism is a barrier to societal progress because it elevates ideas to unquestionable truths. When we cease questioning, we stagnate in our pursuit of truth.

We'll never be entirely free unless we question everything, including religion's core dogmas. But religions resist this.

They wish for us to follow the self-proclaimed interpreters of divine word. To attain complete freedom, we must let go of all religious faith. Our concern should be facts, evidence, objective reality, and demonstrable truths.

We shouldn't merely follow others, regardless of the rituals surrounding them, suggesting greater significance than they possess. True knowledge can only be attained through the freedom to question everything. This is unattainable if we cling to a faith instilled in us from childhood, if we continue to believe in things that defy common sense and scientific understanding.

We must relinquish all forms of spiritual or philosophical authority.

Prominent scientists throughout history have held, and still hold, deep religious convictions. This can make us think that science and religion are two realms that coexist harmoniously within an individual. Religion would deal with moral and transcendent matters, while science would try to understand the natural world around us. This idea of a supposed compatibility and peaceful coexistence between religious faith and reason is mistaken.

I find it mistaken to try and establish separate domains of knowledge, isolated compartments side by side without ever meeting. True knowledge is not about arts or sciences; there's no knowledge of faith and another of reason. Truth is singular, although it can be expressed in various realms, there are not two distinct truths.

Therefore, there can't be two different paths to that truth. What deserves to be called true is not a subjective opinion, but it is based on rational reflection grounded in the scientific method, on facts and evidence, on logical arguments guided by critical thinking. It has nothing to do with accepting irrational dogmas or following supposed religious or any other kind of authorities.

Religion aims to be not only a moral proposition but offers a specific worldview, an interpretation of reality. It posits, in most cases, the existence of supernatural realities like the soul, God, or beings like angels or demons. Religious faith, therefore, completely clashes with scientific assertions.

It is absurd for someone to use the scientific method when conducting physical or biological experiments but refuses to apply that mindset to other central areas of their life.

If we don't believe in a monster in Loch Ness because there's no evidence for its existence, I see no reason why we should believe in the Virgin Mary or Satan. The logical assumption is that all these beings are human-made mythological creations. The only difference between any pseudo-scientific statement and religious beliefs is that the latter are backed by social tradition. That's it. Their essence is the same.

It's contradictory for people who claim to uphold scientific thought to then cling to irrational ideas in other areas of their life. They think that reason should only be concerned with science and outside that domain, all that remains are opinions and relativism. They fail to see the glaring contradiction between championing reason and then venerating a God that contradicts everything we've learned from science over many centuries.

We must be skeptical about everything. Those who are only skeptical about pseudoscience do a disservice to the cause of humanity's rational progress. By their inaction, they allow millions of humans to continue worshipping mythological beings they've created themselves. Everything must undergo critical thinking. Our deepest feelings, political ideologies, art, or religious beliefs. Nothing should escape the scrutiny of reason.

It's also mistaken to believe that understanding opposes feelings, to think that the head and the heart wander different, often opposing, paths. An intelligence that overlooks the emotional dimension of humans, empathy, feelings, is incomplete.

Reason and emotion should walk together since, deep down, they're the same thing. A cold abstract intellect cannot grasp the entire complexity of the human being. And pure emotion, without the support of reason, is doomed as it leads us to irrationality and makes us believe absurdities.

I advocate a moderate skepticism that allows for a rational understanding of the world. Radical skepticism, like Descartes' methodical doubt, denies the possibility of any knowledge, leading to the paralysis of reason. Moderate skepticism, on the other hand, is a healthy intellectual attitude that prevents us from falling into many of irrationality's pitfalls.

Yet, for this skepticism to be complete and therefore genuine, we must apply it to all aspects of human existence, including religion.

Some want to appease both proponents of science and those holding religious beliefs. Hence, they seek intricate conceptual twists to merge oil and water, reason, and faith. In contrast, my goal has never been to please the majority or limit my reasoning to be politically correct. I don't want to please everyone, just to speak the truth. Not my personal truth, which I think is uninteresting, but the rational and objective truth based on a critical analysis of reality.

It's clear to anyone willing to see that faith and reason are at odds. History provides multiple examples of this. Wherever religion is dominant, science is doomed to play a marginal role or even be persecuted. European history offers countless examples supporting this claim.

When we lived under religious domination, and ecclesiastical hierarchies, with the Pope in Rome at the forefront, had immense power over people's lives, science was hindered, marginalized, and harassed for centuries. Galileo serves as an example. Even more striking is the case of Giordano Bruno, a true thought hero murdered by the Catholic Church, sentenced to burn at the stake for his freedom, for daring to think for himself, for challenging absurd religious dogmas.

Faith asserts that the primary source of human knowledge is a supposed revelation from God to men recorded in sacred texts written hundreds or thousands of years ago. Granted, the phenomenon of religion is intricate, and beliefs vary widely. However, I'm referring to the major denominations, such as Christianity, Islam, or Judaism. They rely on a supposed holy book that many even take literally. When God's word has been revealed to humans through prophets or figures like Jesus Christ, anything contradicting it according to its interpreters is deemed heresy. Those challenging these senseless dogmas often face persecution.

It's contradictory to assume that God represents love, mercy, and brotherhood among people, yet some who claim to speak in His name engage in murder, harassment, or insults against those who don't share their beliefs.

This usually happens when someone believes they possess an absolute truth that holds more value than individual human beings. If our life is insignificant compared to the promised eternal life, killing or dying in the name of true faith becomes quite simple.

Many get upset when their religious beliefs are criticized. They view it as a private domain that should remain untouched. The essence is that everyone should believe what they deem fit as long as they don't become fanatical and respect others' convictions. Any criticism of their religion is seen as a severe transgression.

I've mentioned before that I believe everything should be subjected to the test of reason. I don't think anyone should be offended by this stance. If they are, I regret it, but I won't refrain from expressing what I believe to be true.

All religious individuals seem respectable to me. Many talented and morally impeccable people have held and still hold theistic beliefs. This isn't about criminalizing anyone but discussing ideas and determining whether religions represent truth or falsehood. It's about exploring the profound nature of humanity.

This isn't about assaulting anyone, but journeying on the path of wisdom, which always begins within ourselves. Through sincere self-awareness, we can better understand the world we live in.

One cannot seriously discuss the relationship between science and faith without collectively considering the roles each has played throughout history. Notice I say "collectively," meaning in entirety. It's crucial to bear this nuance in mind.

When I criticize religion, some try to counter my views by pointing to the beneficial aspects, like the commendable work done by Caritas, an organization affiliated with the Catholic Church.

This reasoning is flawed as it commits the fallacy of judging a whole based on one of its parts. One cannot assess a person by a single isolated act. Similarly, it's unfair to gauge the role of a complex, millennia-old institution like the Catholic Church by focusing solely on one organization associated with it.

If I were to commit the same error, I could mention the many cases of child sexual abuse that have surfaced in recent decades. It's undoubtedly unjust to blame the vast Catholic community for the despicable actions of a few members.

We shouldn't merely scratch the surface and evaluate religion based only on what affirms our biases. We must reflect on its entire historical role, considering both the good and bad aspects as objectively as possible. To achieve this objectivity, we shouldn't follow shallow, preconceived ideologies. We must approach the topic with a clear, analytical mind.

Many, including educated individuals, belittle science's role. When science is brought up, they often cite its unfortunate outcomes, like the atomic bombs dropped on Hiroshima and Nagasaki at the end of World War II.

Their goal is to highlight that, just as science can heal, it's also used to create devastating weapons that kill millions in moments. They use this as clear evidence of the immense dangers of scientific knowledge.

This line of thinking is flawed for reasons I've mentioned—it judges the whole based on one part. Ultimately, they aim, consciously or unconsciously, to place science and religion on equal footing.

They argue that both can be used for good or ill, so neither can be deemed superior. Such an approach remains superficial and doesn't delve into the core of the matter.

It's evident to me that certain ideologies are intrinsically evil, no matter how they're framed. For instance, I don't believe there's a respectable form of fascism, regardless of its proponents' justifications. Not all ideas hold equal truth.

Fascism is wrong. It doesn't matter if some fascists are wonderful parents or if some defend their right to such beliefs. This ideology opposes democracy's core values and the utmost importance of equality; hence it should always be rejected.

I'm not equating religion to fascism; they're distinct phenomena. My point is that we mustn't remain superficial. When asserting that science can invent weapons—which is true—we must weigh its positive and negative impacts.

No one can deny that scientific knowledge has also produced some monsters. To be fair, we need to weigh all the good and the bad and see where it leans. Only then can we make a proper assessment of the matter examined.

I believe religion is one of humanity's worst creations. It would be best for everyone if it vanished. Its minor positive effects don't come close to outweighing the massive harm it has caused us. Religions are mythological constructs that too many people take as truth. They divert us from the mission of building a more just world with the childish promise of life after death.

We should, therefore, strive for religion to cease and its followers to leave behind these irrational beliefs. Achieving this won't happen overnight. It might never fully happen. Sadly, there will always be those willing to follow others who claim to hold some unattainable supernatural truth.

It's easier for us to deceive ourselves by believing in unreal worlds that we've conjured. Religion mostly operates on an emotional level, which explains the utter lack of its arguments. However, it succeeds in its aim since many are swayed by their basest emotions.

One must be profoundly deluded not to recognize the enormous role science plays in our lives. This is especially evident in medicine. During the Middle Ages, when the Western world was shackled by religion, life expectancy barely touched 30. Child mortality was sky-high; it was tragically common for mothers to die during childbirth or for children not to reach adulthood. Diseases that we've now eradicated plagued those who did survive. Medicine was practically nonexistent, and the few natural remedies were mostly ineffective.

Thanks to science, life expectancy in Europe surged from 30 years a few centuries ago to around 80 now. Child mortality has plummeted. Now, most children grow up to become adults. The enhancements in medicine, living conditions, diet, public sanitation; in essence, the scientific and social progress of humanity is what has led to this monumental advancement.

These milestones weren't achieved by praying or begging some God for aid or adhering to church doctrines that opposed scientific progress for centuries. If we've made these advancements and continue to do so, it's due to the scientific method and the tireless, often unrecognized efforts of countless anonymous scientists dedicated to humanity's well-being.

Comparing what scientific knowledge has given us throughout history, it's evident our species' major advancements happened when we resolutely backed science and free thought.

The decline of religion and the rising prominence of science are intimately connected. We're transitioning from a dark age of blind faith toward an era where reason should dominate.

Unfortunately, this isn't a global trend. Many states, particularly in Arab regions, are dominated by theocracies where faith remains central. When this is the case, freedom suffers, and progress gets stifled by religious directives.

On one side, weigh the vast advancements science has offered, especially in recent centuries. On the other, place the destruction from wars amplified by weapons we never had before.

Clearly, science has given us vastly more than the dark moments like Hiroshima and Nagasaki. Never before have so many enjoyed such high and healthy living standards, all thanks to scientific knowledge and free thought.

This doesn't mean scientists are all saints or that science isn't influenced by non-idealistic factors. Scientists are just like anyone else, with the same flaws. They can be cruel, greedy, narcissistic, seeking only social prestige or profit. This has and will continue to happen.

Remember, some scientists once claimed tobacco wasn't harmful, fully aware of the falsehood. They were, of course, handsomely paid by tobacco companies. There have been scientific frauds and many other reprehensible acts. All of this is true. Yet, the net benefit science has provided is enormous.

Regrettably, many politicians forget this. In most countries, science's role is undervalued. Only a deeply misguided society can act this way. Countries investing in innovation, scientific research, and technological progress enjoy better living standards.

Others treat science and education as secondary. And our politicians often waste public funds on exorbitantly priced infrastructure of questionable value. This is just one of many examples of our missteps. And those speaking against science, including notable religious leaders, are doing society a disservice.

It's essential to recognize the role of science and challenge unscientific views. It's crucial to realize that investing more in scientific research is vital. In the long run, this investment benefits humanity as a whole. Discoveries made in one place eventually find applications everywhere.

Additionally, promoting scientific understanding is critical. It allows the general public to become more familiar with the often complex world of science. Through outreach, the knowledge accumulated over years can become part of the broader cultural understanding. There's still a lot of work to be done in this area. Science, in many ways, needs to be more accessible to society.

I believe that humanity's future lies beyond religious dogmas. Emphasizing science and critical thinking, ultimately valuing freedom, is the way forward. We should avoid blindly following religious doctrines, especially when they claim to have all the answers without evidence. History has shown that dogmatic beliefs can lead to stagnation and repression.

The acceptance of evolution over creationism is a significant achievement for reason against uninformed beliefs. For millennia, it was believed that a deity created us. However, scientific research has shown that humans are just one of millions of species that have existed on Earth. We have evolved from simpler forms of life over time.

Religion often thrives where knowledge is lacking. As scientific understanding grows, the gaps filled by unverified beliefs shrink. Over time, as our knowledge base expands, the role of religion may become less pronounced, paving the way for progress.

There is a fundamental question that science has not yet been able to answer satisfactorily. I'm referring to the question of the origin of the universe. Physics begins a microsecond after the massive explosion called the Big Bang. We still don't understand what caused it. Hence, we must continue to investigate this significant issue. Perhaps one day our understanding of the universe will be deep enough to find an answer.

Religion often illegitimately tries to replace science and provides simplistic answers to complex questions. Most major religions claim that an all-powerful and benevolent God created the universe. As always, they offer no evidence for their claims. Their only foundation is faith in texts written hundreds or thousands of years ago. They know nothing of science, yet they claim to know more than those who dedicate their lives to studying nature.

It's amusing that religion and its followers accuse those of us who champion reason and critical thinking of being arrogant. They say we aim to take the place of God and make other nonsensical claims.

What I find presumptuous is to assert that one possesses the fundamental answers to human existence, claiming to know the universe's origin without providing any objective evidence. Such a stance truly reeks of arrogance. It's more reasonable to admit that we don't have all the answers.

However, people are curious and seek deeper meaning in their lives. Instead of trying to answer these questions themselves, they'd rather have others hand them all the answers.

Another intriguing point is the Christian claim that humans are the ultimate purpose of divine creation. Meaning, everything in the universe was placed there for us.

It seems absurd that such a vast universe exists merely for us to inhabit. If that were the case, I doubt an intelligent deity would create so much matter, stars, and galaxies with no clear purpose, merely as adornments.

This suggests to me that religions primarily display human narcissism. The idea that our tiny planet and our species, just one among millions throughout Earth's history, is the universe's ultimate purpose is nonsensical.

Unfortunately, we like to think we're more special than we truly are. We want to believe an omnipotent God went to great lengths to craft an almost infinite universe just for us.

Any rational person should reject this simplistic worldview. The logical stance is that the universe's creation adheres to natural laws and that our planet's existence is a result of random events. Our existence is the culmination of countless cosmic coincidences. There isn't a guiding hand planning anything, nor is there any hidden meaning that only a supernatural entity can reveal.

Accepting this is challenging. We want to feel unique and central in the universe, yet we're merely a cosmic speck drifting among vast star-filled oceans. Our planet orbits one of countless stars in one of the many galaxies in the universe. We might be the only species on Earth with advanced consciousness, but cosmically speaking, we're rather insignificant. Life's purpose isn't dictated by a higher being. We shape our destiny with our actions.

No hidden agenda is only known to select prophets or enlightened individuals. Our future is collectively determined by our choices. Destiny isn't preordained. Each of us pens our destiny every second of our lives.

The search for meaning is an internal journey. No one can dictate it for us. Life's purpose is evident in our actions, thoughts, relationships, and who we become. Striving for the greater good is a noble aim, beginning with self-awareness, breaking down mental barriers preventing self-understanding, and deeply comprehending our surroundings. Helping others achieve the same contributes to this greater good.

Any effort pushing for human freedom, building a fairer, more compassionate world, and eradicating poverty, violence, and the vast suffering experienced by many is commendable. This should be everyone's life goal. A life dedicated solely to selfish pursuits, accumulating wealth, power, or false prestige, often at others' expense, is senseless.

Outside sources can't grant us a higher purpose in life, though they might show the way. Hence, we won't find life's meaning by following religions, as they force us to betray our rational freedom and subject us to dogma.

Nor will we find the answers by isolating ourselves in monasteries, taking religious vows, following philosophical systems, reading books, or aligning with political parties or ideologies. We'll only find them by thinking independently, being truly free, and using our reason to discern truth from falsehood and right from wrong. This journey is a solo endeavor.

While religion and freethinking often clash, many religious institutions advocate for rational faith. Centuries-old Catholic philosophy traditions support faith based on rational underpinnings, aiming to move beyond mere religious sentimentality and provide solid grounding to faith's truths.

Theologians are right in asserting that rational faith seems more robust than mere religious sentiment. However, in reality, they wrap age-old dogmas in seemingly logical arguments meant to prove the truths faith dictates we should believe. When reason is used this way, it's no longer free; it's subordinated to another purpose.

These "rational" arguments, supposedly proving God's existence but are merely fallacious reasonings, impress many. They give an aura of rationality and false logical solidity. Throughout intellectual history, brilliant minds have tried to bolster faith's truths with notable success.

Reason that's not wholly free to question everything, even itself, is incomplete and bounded by barriers hindering its progress. Religion doesn't want faith and reason to be allies, which is impossible anyway. Religion only wishes to coat itself with a rational veneer to make its baseless dogmas more palatable.

Reason and faith are like oil and water. They can coexist, but they are inherently different. Reason is rooted in absolute freedom, while faith relies on accepting truths that can't be proven.

For two individuals seeking the truth together, both must be willing to revise their prior beliefs if presented with compelling evidence or arguments. This is feasible because reason is subject to the facts and logic. However, when dialoguing with a theist, no matter what's said or what evidence is presented, they'll remain steadfast in their beliefs. Their stance always boils down to "I believe." They won't budge from this position.

Faith is the obstinacy of reason that chooses to cling to a set of truths it cannot prove. We can spend hours discussing with such believers. We can present them with evidence, introduce scientific theories, or lay out logical arguments. Yet none of that will change their minds. This is the fundamental difference between faith and reason, the reason they will always be irreconcilable foes: we either submit to the tribunal of facts or accept religious dogmas. Both cannot coexist simultaneously.

While there are believing scientists, this doesn't refute my point. Such contradictions exist in many people. What I'm pointing out here goes beyond that. I'm discussing the very essence of the matter, its deepest nature.

Science and faith are inherently opposed. When one is strong, the other is weak, and vice versa. The issue is that some people don't embrace the consequences of being fully rational in all their beliefs. They reserve reason for scientific endeavors, but in other areas of their lives, they hold onto beliefs that contradict the scientific method they employ daily. However, this doesn't change the profound incompatibility between these opposing realms of human experience.

Some people are simply afraid of freedom. They fear the ramifications of abandoning their religious beliefs, of facing rejection by family, friends, or the society they inhabit. Accepting the falsehood of religion could label them heretics, pariahs, or social outcasts in a believing environment. It takes courage to confront these consequences.

That's why it's easier to follow the majority, to keep believing what we're supposedly meant to believe—what everyone around us believes. It requires bravery to go against the grain. The path to freedom is never easy. But once embarked upon, there's no turning back. We must always look forward and never stop.

As long as religions exist, conflict will persist. Religion isn't the antidote to the poison of hatred; it's one of its primary sources. Violence is inevitable when individuals believe they possess an absolute truth divinely revealed to them directly or via prophets.

If our earthly existence is just a fleeting moment compared to the eternal life awaiting us after death, then losing it might not seem so significant. Ultimately, the only thing that matters is earning an eternal reward beside the God we serve. The leap to fanaticism is short, and tragically, countless individuals throughout history have died or been killed by those claiming to act on God's behalf.

This highlights one of the many contradictions in religions. They preach love and universal brotherhood while simultaneously fostering hatred and division.

Religious violence manifests in various forms, not just through burnings at the stake or terrorist acts by religious fanatics. Violence has more subtle, complex facets. Beyond its most overt displays, many religions perpetrate less explicit forms of violence.

If a parent emotionally manipulates their children into adopting their religious beliefs, that's also violence. When major religions criticize and criminalize homosexuals, they're exerting violence upon this community. Claiming, as Catholicism does, that sexuality's sole purpose is reproduction and branding any other relationships as sinful is nonsensical. Denying homosexuals the right to marry, a right heterosexual couples enjoy, is also violence.

Many have taken their lives because a religion's moral code made them feel wicked merely due to a non-mainstream sexual orientation. Some marry just to keep up appearances, condemning their partners to a counterfeit life and a love that can never be whole. This has caused immense pain for countless individuals over centuries.

I'd also like to address the violence major religions inflict upon women. This happens when they're told their primary role in life is motherhood, or when they're denied priesthood and given a marginal role within religious hierarchies. These too are acts of violence.

It's clear to anyone willing to see that religions haven't fostered gender equality; quite the opposite. They've significantly bolstered a patriarchal model, marginalizing half the world's population—a trend that persists. This is the grievous violence religions often perpetrate.

We must ardently combat the violence that plagues humanity. Religions, instead of aiding this noble cause, have done the exact opposite. They've been a source of conflict, war, division, pain, and suffering. I oppose religions because I believe we can build a better world without them.

However, to achieve this, we must gradually free ourselves from mental shackles, from centuries-old lies ingrained in our psyche. By accepting death as an inevitable part of life, religion largely becomes redundant, allowing us to genuinely focus on improving our society.

Following others is easy, especially when they claim to have a magical, supernatural truth explaining life's profound meaning. But we shouldn't let others think for us. We should be free—in the truest, deepest sense—to find our answers and strive for a better world.

SECTS DESTROY YOUR FREEDOM

I don't believe there's any organization more toxic to free thought than a cult, as it suppresses the individual and places them in service to an organization, leader, or guru. Therefore, speaking of "destructive cults" is redundant. Every cult erodes the freedom of its followers, though there may be varying degrees of toxicity between them.

The distinction between a cult and a religion is blurry. Many of today's recognized religions were once viewed as cults. Similarly, established religions like Christianity or Islam contain within them groups that are clearly cultish, employing mind control techniques similar to those used by cults.

Furthermore, I believe that individuals deeply committed to religions, such as priests, monks, and other laypeople, lead lives identical to those in cultic groups.

In doctrinal aspects, there's no difference between a religion and a cult. Although some cults don't have a defined doctrine, like commercial groups that merely foster the financial greed of their followers.

Members of the Church of Scientology believe that Xenu, a dictator from the Galactic Confederacy, brought billions of people to Earth in spaceships 75 million years ago. Allegedly, he dropped them around volcanoes and annihilated them with hydrogen bombs.

This bizarre story is as hard to believe as the concept of an all-powerful God impregnating a human virgin, having a son who is himself, and sending him on a doomed mission preaching a doctrine (while also walking on water, raising the dead, and healing the possessed) to ultimately be crucified, resurrected three days later, and ascend to heaven.

Both narratives are equally fantastical. The only difference is that we're more accustomed to the latter due to our upbringing and the Christian culture that permeates Western civilization.

Religious and cultic doctrines share characteristics. Their main feature is their unverifiability. This sets them apart from science, which is based on objective evidence. Religious narratives can't be proven, only accepted. You either take them or leave them. There's no objective evidence of their truth. All we have are testimonies and stories, most of which come from unreliable sources.

Their core beliefs are unchanging. There might be alterations in superficial aspects, but the foundational beliefs remain static. Since religious narratives are detached from reality, no evidence or discovery alters their core ideas. This is one of many reasons why theology isn't a science, even though it's taught in some universities. In fact, they often contradict much of our scientific knowledge. The resurrection of the dead goes against everything we know about human biology after centuries of study.

The fundamental difference between "religion" and "cult" is this: followers of a religion don't undergo a radical transformation in their lives or personalities simply by adhering to a specific faith. They might have beliefs or partake in rituals, but their religious ideas aren't the center of their existence.

Someone who is Catholic, attends Mass on Sundays, baptizes their children, and follows the moral doctrine of the Church is not in a cult. However, within the Catholic Church (and all religions) there are cultic groups. In cults, which are typically smaller, it's uncommon to find what we might call "external followers"; the majority are core members. Cults might have a hierarchy or varying levels of commitment to the organization.

Those who join a cult lose their freedom, even if they joined voluntarily. Their critical thinking and worldview are transformed by the fervent belief that they possess absolute truth. This supposed truth is the exclusive property of the organization or its leader.

In this respect, there's no difference between religions and cults. Nearly all religions claim to be the true one, implying that others are false. Hence, conflicts are inevitable.

Although leaders of various faiths talk of peace and respect between beliefs, history shows us that confrontations between them are frequent, something still true today. The unification of all religions is impossible since most view themselves as the only true one. This suggests, in my opinion, that it's most likely all are false.

A cult member undergoes a radical transformation in their identity. This is what usually alerts their family and friends that something is amiss. This change isn't instant; it requires a process of mental indoctrination that can last months or years, often spanning a lifetime without the member realizing it.

Cults nullify rationality. The follower's thought process is replaced by the doctrine imposed by the group and its leader.

Many of these organizations talk about freedom and self-discovery. In reality, they enslave individuals, turning them into cogs in a machine. The collective is what's important, not the individual members.

Within this cultic context, members might do things they would never do outside this insulated world. They might even kill, steal, or cover up heinous crimes, like child sexual abuse, to protect the organization. The group, as the holder of supreme truth, is all that matters. If lying or harming others protects it, then so be it. The collective or the leader is the only priority.

Most people suffer. And I don't just mean from physical ailments, diseases, unemployment, or other social issues. Many suffer silently because they find life meaningless, everything seeming grim and void of interest. Amid this darkness, people seek answers and guidance.

This is the ideal environment for such groups. The more suffering and chaos, the more desperate we become. Those who thrive on fear can then peddle their hope, offering a higher purpose to suffering and deploying their mind control methods to dominate others.

Millions are condemned to social marginalization. In a cult, however, everyone has a place. Even without money or education, one can perform auxiliary tasks, like cleaning group facilities.

Cults promote fraternal bonds, making lonely individuals mistakenly believe they've found a family. These groups exploit personal vulnerabilities to gain control. They don't wish to help; they want to use us.

Inside a cult, any inner turmoil is replaced by a simplistic dichotomy: us and them, good and evil. The group represents freedom, the only path to happiness: the ultimate good. Everything outside is evil, a threat.

That terror of "the others," of what's outside, is constantly encouraged by the cult leaders. They even instill phobias in their followers, making them pathologically afraid to leave the group. They're told that they'll fall into the hands of Satan, become drug addicts and murderers, their children will be stillborn, and they will burn in hell for all eternity under terrible punishments, and so on.

Fear is the tool that ensures unwavering loyalty to the leader and the doctrine. The looming threat squashes any internal criticism, since dissenters can be accused of being tools of rival groups wanting to destroy the organization.

It's common for cults, regardless of their type, to anticipate some horrific event: the end of times, the arrival of an alien ship that will annihilate us, a global nuclear war, a massive plague that will exterminate everyone (except for the cult members), and so forth. They also promote conspiracy theories and make up powerful enemies, claiming, for instance, that the Antichrist or another organization is out to get them, or that the government is after them. This justifies the cult's secretive and militaristic nature.

Another key trait in cults and religions is the perpetual hope for something better than what we currently have. This concept of waiting for a better future is used to dominate believers in the present.

They await the arrival of an alien ship that will take us to a wondrous planet, the Final Judgment and the resurrection of the dead, or a paradise beyond death where perfect happiness awaits. And if the promised utopia fails to materialize, leaders can blame their followers: "We haven't succeeded because of you; that's why we need to work harder." It's all about instilling irrational fear and guilt.

Many cults even have a set date for the end of the world. The Jehovah's Witnesses, for example, have predicted this apocalypse multiple times, without ever being right. Some of these organizations claim it will all end in five years. When that doesn't happen, they set a new date and so on.

The goal is to instill fear. They aim to control their followers by claiming they have some superior knowledge that will help them overcome the impending catastrophe they prophesy, a knowledge exclusive to the group and its leaders.

There's no free thinking in a cult. Members believe they're acting on their own, but they're just following a doctrine imposed by others, parroting what's been thought by the leaders or the creators of the ideology. That's why dialogue with them is impossible.

Dialogue isn't just an exchange of ideas. Genuine dialogue implies the possibility of mutual agreement, with both sides willing to adjust their initial stances if they rationally find them flawed. The purpose of dialogue should be to find the truth.

However, the cultist isn't searching for anything. They already believe they know the ultimate truth. Their aim is to share it, gain more followers, and increase the organization's power. They don't want to engage with us; they want to convert us.

We could talk for hours with them, and make no progress. They're even trained to hold these kinds of conversations with "non-believers," repeating the same ideas over and over. There's nothing original in what they say. If they see they won't achieve their conversion goal, they leave. They can't waste time on anything not serving the cult's interests.

Members of a cultic group live under the dominion of the organization's leaders, often without realizing it. There's an unhealthy devotion and personality cult around the leader. The leader becomes everything—God's instrument, the embodiment of good, the one teaching the only possible truth. Followers might even kill or die for them without hesitation.

The cult aims to be its members' only family, their true family. They want to make them believe that only they care and understand them. Emotional bonds between members are strengthened by isolating them from their regular surroundings, taking them far away to a different city or country, making the follower feel lonely and disoriented.

It's indicative that many priests or nuns refer to themselves as "father" or "mother," trying to mimic the family relationship they want to establish within their community.

This is one of the most commonly used mind control techniques by cults. The follower breaks away from their biological family and adopts a new "family," leading to a conflict between the cult and the biological family.

Those who have fought most against the cult phenomenon are the families of those involved. For many parents, a child's involvement in such a group feels like a total loss of the child they deeply cared for. Adding to their pain is hearing their child claim to join "of their own free will," exercising their freedom. But that's far from the truth.

Someone who has undergone such intense indoctrination has their ability to choose greatly diminished. Thus, for them to successfully leave the group, they need a deprogramming treatment carried out by specialists to restore their original lost personality due to the indoctrination they've experienced.

Many are struck by the absurdity of the beliefs of these groups: "How can anyone believe they telepathically communicate with aliens who will come to fetch us in a flying saucer?" some wonder. "Those people are crazy," others claim. But they're neither crazy nor dumb. Many cult members are intellectually sharp.

So, how can someone educated believe such outlandish things? We could say the same about established religions: how can a doctor, someone who knows the human body, believe in Jesus' resurrection? Yet many do.

The crux of the matter is that religions and cults operate on an emotional level. We believe because we want to, as these beliefs fulfill basic needs in our lives, even if they defy reason.

Something that strongly resonates with cult followers is the idea that they've been chosen, that they've received a "call" to fulfill an extraordinary mission that will change the fate of humanity. They believe they're the vanguard of a major transformation. They dream that in the future, all of humanity will worship their leaders and build monuments in their honor, and that the followers will be admired for being the first to understand the ultimate truth. They elevate their leaders to the stature of great historical figures, with many delusionally believing they are the new messiah.

It's paradoxical that organizations that speak of brotherhood, love, and family, disdain their members, exploiting and stripping away their dignity and freedom. All that matters is the group. Sacrifices, lies, even suicides or killings can be justified if the leader demands it.

Everything a follower possesses is fully at the group's disposal: their body, time, money, even their life. Nothing belongs to the individual anymore. The organization controls it all. The human being is no longer an end but a means.

Cults use unique expressions and concepts to set themselves apart and create a collective identity, isolating themselves. They often adopt a similar appearance: dressing alike, even mimicking each other's gestures. They might shave their heads, grow their hair or beard long, wear robes, or suits and ties. Some adopt dress codes based on their organizational rank.

It's common for members to change their names within the group, signaling a new phase and identity, thus forming a personality shaped by the leader for the follower. All these tactics are used to strengthen the group and suppress individuality, ensuring members identify with the group identity.

Reinforcing indoctrination often involves prayer, mantras, songs, or reciting religious texts. This disrupts independent thought, hindering critical thinking. Followers shouldn't think but merely repeat what's been taught. This way, they reinforce the doctrine, expelling any doubts or thoughts against the group. Many cults teach their followers to chant phrases or songs whenever they feel doubt or believe they're being tempted by evil.

One characteristic of cult members is their enthusiasm for the doctrine, organization, and especially the leaders. They're energetically committed, showing exaggerated zeal. They may work tirelessly for days on end without expecting anything in return.

When these organizations engage in business activities—and many do for funding—they're formidable competitors. Their members work exhaustively for free. It's hard for legitimate businesses to compete with them, hence many cults amass significant power and build economic empires.

Sectarian mental programming is reinforced through ceremonies and rites designed to solidify group power and the leaders' positions. Ascending ranks often involve tests and initiation rituals to reinforce loyalty. Members make pledges, swearing blind obedience.

The organization takes over every aspect of our lives, even intimate ones like sexuality. They dictate whom we should marry, how many children to have, and so forth. Sex becomes another control instrument.

Some cults lure male members using women, and some even force women into prostitution for funds. It's not uncommon for male leaders to engage with any female members they wish. One's standing in the group often correlates with closeness to the leader.

Controlling sexuality might involve enforced celibacy, ensuring members' assets go to the group. Non-compliers live in fear of discovery, hypocritically advocating for abstinence while not practicing it.

Cults demand blind obedience. They don't educate but rather inculcate strict compliance. They resemble armies. Leaders are omniscient, and followers must obey without question. A sense of war with the outside world justifies this martial regime, where criticism equals treachery.

No organization can lead us to truth. The journey to knowledge is personal. No religion, cult, or philosophy can replace this personal journey. They all ultimately distort the truth, seeking more power, followers, and especially wealth.

Such groups exemplify deeply rooted societal issues and human flaws: desiring guidance, seeking easy answers to hard questions, and a longing to belong. Cults isolate from the world, blaming it for all evils. They create miniature totalitarian societies where a few exploit the majority using fear and manipulation.

The freedom we yearn for will never be found within a cult or church. Only deep self-understanding can free our minds. Recognizing our innermost fears and anxieties can transform them into creativity and motivation to improve our surroundings.

We'd then never wish to join any group or heed immoral individuals exploiting others' insecurities. We should resist those demanding obedience and adoration in the name of revealed truths. Overcoming fear makes free thinking possible.

FEAR OF DEATH

Imagine the person you hold most dear in this world. Be it our mother or father, a sibling, a child, a spouse or partner. Occasionally, these profound connections are abruptly and unexpectedly severed with the harsh arrival of death. This inflicts a profound pain that shadows us throughout life, weighing on us like a heavy burden.

The loss of a loved one leaves scars so deep and painful that only time can somewhat alleviate, but they remain with us for the rest of our days. Everyone, at one point or another, will face this heartbreak. And when it does happen, our tears and sadness are so overpowering that it feels like we're shattering from within.

In these dreadful moments, when life can seem absurd and meaningless, we yearn for answers to this debilitating pain which plunges us into the abyss of despair. We look for an escape, something to ease our sorrow.

That's when religion steps in. Many, who in their daily lives overlook religious phenomena and live detached from them, find solace in religion during these devastating times, when faced with death.

"Fear not," say followers of the myriad churches and faiths across the world, "that person whom you love and cherish hasn't truly died, but waits for you in the afterlife, longing for your reunion."

This simple message wields an incredible power. It's a seed that easily takes root in the human heart. No fear is more profound and primal than the fear of death.

Everyone knows that someday, they must confront the end of their life. And at that moment, neither wealth nor power amassed over a lifetime can save us from this inevitable fate. Every time we witness another's death, especially that of a close one, it's a reflection of our own mortality.

It isn't love that fuels religion or bestows upon it its immense allure. Instead, it's fear, the desire for eternal life, the quest for meaning in a life that will end eventually. Religion offers psychological comfort, solace at life's end, and a way to cope with the loss of loved ones.

Yet, there's a hefty price to pay. We surrender to irrationality, to blind faith that renounces the reason that makes us human. We become slaves to dogmas crafted by supposed enlightened men seeking to control others.

We must confront the harsh reality of death head-on. Without understanding it, we can't truly grasp the essence of religion or the profound nature of humanity. Some irresponsibly mock religious imagery, oblivious to its captivating power. We're dealing with a fundamental aspect of human existence. Remember, a vast majority across the globe believe in something supernatural.

We must set aside all biases, any ideology aiming to oversimplify the intricate phenomenon of religion. Mere historical perspectives, comparative religious studies, or origin analyses aren't enough.

We want to delve deeper, understand the very essence of religion and the psychological drivers behind it. And this can't be achieved through a purely intellectual or historical lens.

To understand religion is to understand human essence. Without introspection, our understanding remains shallow, offering an incomplete, thus misleading explanation.

Why do we grieve when a loved one passes away? This phenomenon warrants careful contemplation. Understanding its intricacies can unlock insights into religion.

Love is often a form of attachment. A bond, a feeling of wholeness in the presence of a loved one. It's an emotion hard to capture in words. It's seen in the eyes of young lovers, the embrace between a father and child on a birthday, the feeling when a mother holds her newborn. We're at peace around our loved ones.

However, when death strikes, joy turns to melancholy. Past smiles transform into tears.

We fight tooth and nail against death. In sickness, we seek the best medical help, turning to any possible savior from the inevitable. And when death does arrive, we search for someone to blame, often those who promised assistance. Accepting the end is hard, and its arrival brings immense frustration and anger.

We yearn for answers, a way to conquer the grim reaper who's snatched away our beloved. Attachment has us clinging to the past, cherishing moments with the departed. Memories, or anything that reminds us of them, amplify our pain.

Some hide away photos of the deceased, attempting to keep their memory from surfacing constantly. Those unable to move on condemn themselves to eternal mourning.

As time passes, pain diminishes. Forgetfulness buries painful memories, but the scar remains, because we never truly confronted death. We're haunted by this pain, secretly hoping for a reunion in an afterlife.

To truly address death, we must let go of the past, cherish the present, and be free from yesterday's memories. This doesn't mean forgetting, but detaching mentally from a time that won't return. Only by living in the present can we prevent the past from hurting us.

We cannot alter what's gone. While cherished moments with others no longer exist, they prevent us from fully embracing the present if we wallow in self-pity, dwelling on those forever lost. When we let go of the past, we are reborn into the present, liberated from anxieties of a nonexistent future. This is the path to true happiness.

Yet, we resist this. We wish our deceased loved ones were somewhere, waiting to be reunited, to relive those precious emotions. We hope for a future reminiscent of a rosier past.

How does the human mind cope? By storytelling. We're myth-making creatures. Imagination is undeniably a core facet of intelligence. Not inherently bad, it lets us revel in wonderful tales, novels, and poetry. It turns toxic when we mistake fiction for reality.

Our fear of death compels us to create myths to conquer it. We envision wondrous heavens and terrifying hells, places of reward or punishment, where death is defeated by eternal life, where pain ceases. We conjure the myth of reincarnation, the concept of the soul, resurrection, and myriad intricate fantasies. In essence, these are answers to our deep-seated fear of the inevitable end.

Religions have evolved to an extraordinary level of sophistication in their fantasies. We're told about ghosts, peculiar beings like devils, angels, and all sorts of supernatural entities. There would be nothing wrong with these beliefs if they stayed within the realm of literature. Sadly, they become fictions revered by millions, icons we place on pedestals, and for which some are willing to die or kill. This is one of the primary distortions of religion. It insists that fantasy supersedes reality.

World churches have been built not on the foundations of love, but on the fear of our own death and the hope for an eternal life where suffering ends forever. The success religion has achieved may be the most significant testament to the deep irrationality that grips most humans. It shows how our feelings, fears, and desires ultimately drive us to believe in things that contradict everything we know about the world around us.

If we don't confront the issue of death, we will never understand the essence of religion. From that understanding should come the abandonment of all religious beliefs. When we grasp the meaning of this phenomenon, realizing it's merely a mental escape from the problem of death, our ignorance, and the many uncertainties that haunt us, not just intellectually but deeply within our core, we realize how absurd it is to cling to childish beliefs.

To be mature is to accept life's hardships, to embrace death as a natural part of our existence, and not to seek meaningless escapes. However, most of humanity prefers to live as children needing guidance from others in their search for truth.

Death ceases to be a problem when we accept it as an inherent part of life, our inevitable fate. If we acknowledge it for what it is, then we don't need to invent escapes; we just need to live the best we know how because this is the only life there is.

Avoiding a problem, which is what we do when adopting religious beliefs, doesn't resolve our anxieties. The pain remains, lurking, ready to resurface at any moment. But if we face the problem of death, without inventing alternate realms or ideas like souls and reincarnation, if we can look death in the eye and see our own reflection, acknowledging it as part of our existence, that's when it stops troubling us, and religion becomes a hollow, meaningless social ritual.

I began this reflection talking about the pain of losing a close loved one. One might wonder: how can we overcome such a death without religion's aid? This is undoubtedly a crucial question we must address.

To many, life seems bleak and empty. They feel it's pointless to be born, work for decades in a job they don't enjoy, and then die. They hope for something more beautiful after death, a world without pain, where good triumphs over the dark forces of evil.

This belief is profoundly mistaken. It holds us back from working to our fullest potential to improve society. The pain and misery we see are reflections of our inner state. The world is cruel and violent because many people are. We are the world. We created society. But instead of owning up to our creation, we escape into religion, fantasizing about an eternal life.

When you accept that death is the end and realize that this life is all we have, making it incredibly precious, everything around you changes.

I'm not speaking of intellectual understanding, like solving a math problem, but a deep, experiential realization of its meaning. Once we achieve this level of understanding, accepting death becomes not an abstract idea but a foundational worldview.

The moment we fully accept the finiteness of human existence, every moment becomes unique, every second precious, because there won't be another reality after death to build a perfect society. This life, this world, which many waste by harming others and themselves, is all we have and is the most precious treasure.

Denying an afterlife and religion doesn't lead to sadness. Instead, it's the best way to cope with the loss of loved ones and the fear many have of their own death. Every beginning has an end. We must accept that end to truly value what we are. It's a mistake to deceive ourselves into thinking we'll reunite with departed loved ones someday.

By doing so, the scars from such losses never fully heal; they're open wounds that bleed continuously as long as we cling to the hope of a reunion that won't occur. Accepting the death of those we've loved doesn't mean we stop loving them. It makes the memories of times shared truly irreplaceable and unique. That's why it's vital to stop daydreaming about fantastic worlds and appreciate the beauty around us, fully experiencing life's precious moments.

One might wonder how I'm so certain death is the end, that all that remains are memories and the impacts we've made. To me, it's baffling that so many people refuse to see the obvious and cling to the uncertain hope of eternal life.

What happens when someone dies is apparent to us all. Their body decomposes, returning to nature, and that person ceases to exist. We can continue to believe otherwise, refusing to accept the evident. Those are just escapisms, signs of our fragility.

After thousands of years, nowhere in the world has objective evidence been found to show that there's any form of life beyond physical death. And I don't believe such evidence will ever be found. What's really happening is painfully straightforward, even though many choose to turn a blind eye and continue to nurture irrational beliefs.

We fear death. We want to live forever; we wish the people we love could always be by our side. And because of that, we invent supernatural worlds.

Religion is a form of self-deception. It's an escape that leads nowhere. Moreover, it's a dangerous escape because it prevents us from confronting the reality of death head-on. By letting the false hopes of eternal life distract us from the immense task of transforming our world, we're veering off the true path that will allow us to build a better future for all.

Let's not fear death. We need to accept it as the natural end of every life. Let's stop taking refuge in false hopes, dreaming of impossible reunions. Let's fight with all our might to try to improve our surroundings. Let's savor every moment, every second. Our time is limited. There are no second chances. Life is lived only once, which is why we have the tremendous responsibility to do something worthwhile with it.

When we overcome the distress caused by death through understanding, religion becomes irrelevant, an empty narrative that contributes nothing to our lives. The belief in eternal existence is a human mind's fantasy, an imperfect answer to our inability to accept the end as a natural outcome of every life.

Evidence that religion and death are closely intertwined can be seen in the fact that churches worldwide are often filled with older people, those nearing the end of their life. Many spend much of their lives indifferent to religion. They claim to be believers, yet their actions contradict the very beliefs they profess. They speak of love for God, but they go to war, kill others, steal, and act in greedy and cruel ways. However, when they feel the looming presence of death, they turn to religion, seeking an answer to that inevitable end.

Rather than facing what they've done, it's easier to dream of eternal life, confess, say some empty prayer, and plead for divine forgiveness. In doing so, they're looking for a way out. They're unwilling to own up to their mistakes and are fearful that their life has been devoid of virtue, meaningless. They want another shot. They hope for forgiveness and want to be relieved of the anxiety caused by death.

All of this is in vain. However, it's much easier than facing the truth, than admitting that life ends and perhaps we haven't used ours as we should have. This fear feeds religion and has allowed many religious institutions to amass vast material wealth. The false sense of security they offer isn't free. We pay a steep price for it, and many use it to establish their dominion over others, to build powerful organizations.

I'm confident that if humans were immortal, religion would play a marginal role. It's our inability to accept our finite nature, to come to terms with death, that fuels and propels the phenomenon of religion. Even though the Earth has been around for millions of years, we know that one day, far in the future, it too will vanish. The Sun, which facilitated life on our planet, will eventually obliterate our Solar System. The world as we know it will cease to exist. And it's likely that the universe, with its billions of galaxies, will, in a time frame almost inconceivable to us, cease to exist as well.

It makes no sense to believe that humans, who are but a tiny speck in the vast cosmic ocean, could live forever. When we realize our own finitude and our cosmic insignificance, we see that we're just a small part of an immeasurable universe we barely understand. Eternity is a construct of our limited human mind—a lofty dream we cling to because we can't accept the inevitable end that awaits us.

DYING FOR SOCIETY

The family is where an individual truly takes shape, more than in a school, college, or university. It's our parents who instill religious beliefs in us, passing down our affiliation to a particular faith. If they are Christian or Muslim, for example, it's likely that we'll be too, because children usually inherit their parents' religious views.

I've always believed that education should be grounded in freedom, letting the young ones choose their path. While guidance is crucial, they should bear the responsibility of making their own decisions.

Unfortunately, most parents don't see it this way. They believe that upbringing means ensuring their children embrace their own beliefs. If they're Christian, for instance, they'll send their kids to schools that propagate those beliefs and values. They'll baptize them following their religious rituals, hoping they'll adopt the same faith.

Everyone desires their parents' approval and pride in their accomplishments. We don't want to let them down. We seek their validation, comfort, love, and affection.

Sadly, behind these sentiments often lies a cruelty, especially when considering the role of religion within the family setting.

Imagine a deeply devout family, regardless of the specific religion—most act similarly in this context. This family will undoubtedly do everything to ensure their children adopt their beliefs, practices, and join the same religious community. They'll monitor any deviations from the "true path" and will send them to schools where they're continuously indoctrinated.

This indoctrination process usually works. Growing up in a Muslim society, surrounded by a Muslim family, attending a Muslim school, and being raised as a Muslim, for example, makes it challenging to challenge this predetermined path.

However, in rare instances, some break free. These individuals, due to certain circumstances and through a courageous act of free will, reject the faith imposed upon them since childhood.

When this happens, society's induced mental enslavement becomes apparent. Parents are left heartbroken. Our mothers weep, our fathers grieve over their "ungrateful" child. They try persuading us back to their faith, urging us to abandon atheism or any newfound belief differing from theirs.

This common scenario in many households unveils the horrors of religion. In a heavily theistic society, we aren't granted the freedom to choose. From birth, religious biases are imposed upon us, and societal pressures push for their acceptance. Rejecting our parents' faith often comes at a high emotional cost. In extreme cases, some are disowned by their families for their choices.

This boils down to emotional blackmail, a form of psychological manipulation. Some parents are only willing to love their children as long as they hold onto the same beliefs and views as them. From a young age, they set a path for their children to follow, and if the children stray from it, they're punished. They're told they're a disappointment, a source of sadness, the shame of the family, that they're wrong. The parents argue they've worked hard for their children their entire lives, and the children repay them with ingratitude and betrayal.

That's why many people resort to hypocrisy. They continue to participate in family religious rituals, baptizing their children, marrying in a church or according to the religious ceremony of their confession. They lead lives of believers, but deep down, they don't believe in the religion they claim to follow. They're scared of the fallout that might occur if they were to publicly voice their true thoughts and feelings. They prefer a life of deceit rather than fully facing the implications of their beliefs, or their lack of faith in their parents' religion.

How do people handle this? Most choose to sidestep the issue. They accept religion as a family legacy without even questioning what they believe in. They avoid conflict and, even though they don't truly believe in the religion they claim to belong to, they'd rather keep up appearances and enjoy the support of the group. In this way, they can continue to retain their loved ones' affection, even though deep down they think that all those religious ideas are just meaningless myths.

Living like that may indeed be convenient, but it's nothing but a facade. If we don't fully confront the implications of our beliefs, there'll always be an inner pain, a conflict we might try to ignore but remains present even if we turn a blind eye. A hypocritical existence is false, and therefore, without real value. It's the life of someone who remains enslaved by others.

That's why, when some gather enough courage to confess their beliefs or lack of faith to their families, that process is seen as liberating, and few regret taking that step. We should lead lives consistent with our beliefs, aligned with who we are, avoiding a dissonance between thought and action. Being free is always more desirable than the deceitful comfort of following societal conventions.

The curious thing about this entire matter is that many of these individuals who cling to their faith deep down don't know much about it. They haven't reflected upon their religion and lack an in-depth understanding of their own beliefs. They've simply embraced a certain faith out of tradition or societal influence. There hasn't been any prior introspection.

Moreover, at no point in their lives have they freely chosen to accept their family's religion. They merely do what they believe they should, just like almost everyone around them. Unbeknownst to them, they are slaves to the group, to the authority society wields over us all.

There are numerous ways to arrive at the same destination. Sometimes, the crucial difference isn't the destination itself but the path we tread to get there. This notion can be applied to various facets of life, including religion. Someone might accept a particular faith out of tradition. However, if they delve into its history, doctrines, and beliefs, they might develop a profound understanding of it, undoubtedly strengthening their convictions. Likewise, one can resist societal authority and adopt a religion or atheism out of personal initiative, rather than following the masses. While these journeys may lead to the same end, they are fundamentally different.

Undoubtedly, the weakest faith is that which is promoted by societal authority. It's a tradition that can be discarded when it no longer serves a purpose or brings benefits. Far stronger is religious belief that stems from an intense internal process of reflection about one's convictions. Such introspection doesn't necessarily lead to an affirmation of the religion but could instead lead to its rejection.

However, when we chart our course out of personal conviction, we follow it with much greater determination and belief than when it's laid out for us by others.

Regrettably, most people don't wish to ponder what they believe or delve into their deepest convictions. It's easier to go with the flow, to follow others, to do what one assumes they should. Many lack the interest, ability, or desire to question what they're told to believe.

When this happens, freedom becomes a mirage, a hollow illusion that deceives us into thinking our ideas are our own when they truly belong to others. We merely parrot what society dictates we should believe, becoming echoes of ideas that aren't genuinely ours.

Let's delve deeper into this reflection on the relationship between religion and society. We initially focused on the family. However, the significance of religious phenomena undoubtedly transcends this limited scope. Religion is more than just a family tradition; it's a societal feature and an identifying mark for many human groups. Additionally, there's a strong connection between political power and ecclesiastical hierarchies.

Imagine an ambitious politician aiming for the highest echelons of power. What must they do to achieve this? Should they always voice their true thoughts, being candid with potential voters? Unfortunately, it's clear that they shouldn't. Doing so exposes them to the risk of rejection. Hence, they're compelled to hide views that might upset the majority. When we desperately seek social endorsement, we become prisoners to others. We aren't free to express our beliefs because we fear ostracism.

If someone aspires to have a stellar political career in the United States or any other country where religion holds sway, they must profess a faith and embrace a religious creed, even if they don't genuinely believe in it. Failing to do so, or voicing an opinion that contrasts with the majority's stance on this matter, will undoubtedly terminate their political aspirations.

If we pause and contemplate this issue, its absurdity becomes evident. We aren't concerned about whether the politician is competent, educated, honest, or hard-working. The majority is merely fixated on them adhering to a series of senseless societal conventions. Those who dare challenge these norms face group ostracization and its associated wrath.

In a tolerant society, the philosophical convictions individuals hold about religion shouldn't matter. It's irrelevant whether they're believers or not, whether they're Christian, Muslim, agnostic, or atheist. We should judge individuals based on their ability to fulfill a role and their potential to contribute to society's collective good.

Yet, this isn't the reality. The majority behave as they do within their families. That is, they want politicians to mirror their own image. If they're Christian, they want a Christian politician. If they're Muslim, they'd vote for a Muslim representative. All of this is irrational, as religious beliefs (or the lack thereof) shouldn't play a pivotal role in the decisions a public representative must make concerning collective management.

But all of this is of little concern to us. What we want is for that person representing us to reflect as much as possible who we are, our beliefs and habits. It's quite disheartening, especially during elections, to see politicians trying to be seen in places frequented by the majority. For instance, if people enjoy football, they make sure to appear in a place of honor in the stadium box to be seen enjoying the match. Perhaps many of them aren't even interested in the sport, but that doesn't matter. The key here is to convey the often false impression that politicians share the same interests as the general public.

I have no doubt that many people who fervently cling to religion, attending Sunday mass with their families and Bibles in hand, would abandon these beliefs if they weren't socially beneficial. What matters to them isn't the truth of their faith, but its social utility.

They haven't even considered whether Catholicism is the only true religion or if reincarnation exists, as some branches of Buddhism claim. Many don't even take their own beliefs seriously, living their lives in ways that betray the very religions they claim to follow.

All of this is a grand deception. A socially accepted hypocrisy. Many presidents of major countries claim to be religious. They entertain pastors in their influential offices, read the Bible or other sacred books, and pray on Sundays before family meals. They're full of righteous talk, discussing God, good and evil, and professing devotion.

These same people, who often look down on those without religious convictions, won't hesitate to start wars, sending our children to die for their own ambitions. They talk about the love of God but exhibit profound disregard for the lives of those doomed to obey them. Blinded by greed, ambition, and thirst for power, they nevertheless insist they're devout believers.

Any rational individual should ponder these issues and wonder how people continue to support politicians who claim religiousness while merely exploiting religion for selfish aims. If these admired leaders weren't sheer hypocrites, they wouldn't wage wars or allow indoctrination to breed blind obedience.

These politicians would advocate for the common good, for the vulnerable, striving for fairer and more compassionate societies. If they were truly religious, they'd believe all humans are children of a single God, each person unique and deserving of respect. Yet, after praying in church, they don't hesitate to order killings or start wars.

There's a deep link between religion and politics, between the throne and the altar. Since time immemorial, they've been intertwined. So much so that many political leaders have concurrently been religious leaders. Even in ancient Egypt, pharaohs were deemed gods.

In Europe, there's a long-standing tradition of the Catholic Church aligning with the various kingdoms that have ruled the continent over centuries. The power elite want to control the populace, preserving their privileges and the social order that favors them. Religion serves this purpose well.

Firstly, it aids political leaders in asserting their position and supremacy over others. Just as there's a God in heaven, there should be an earthly king chosen by divine mandate. The earthly hierarchy mirrored the celestial order where the true God ruled the world with absolute power.

This supreme deity was, in turn, accompanied by a heavenly court of angels and other powerful supernatural entities devoted to His service. This paralleled the nobility supporting the monarch. Then, at the bottom of this social pyramid, were the common folk, who could only hope to be ruled by the king and his nobles.

Clearly, this worldview we see in Christianity and many other religions is a human invention. It's a justification for an unjust social order. We've lived for thousands of years in totalitarian, unequal, non-democratic societies. That's why all this religious mythology reflects the unfair society that created it.

I have no doubt that religion has been an obstacle, making it more difficult to build more open, free, and democratic societies. Almost all tyrants in history, from absolute monarchs to military dictatorships—with the exception of communist regimes—have used it as a tool for social control.

There's another key reason why religion has been useful for political power. I refer to the fact that it helps people come to terms with the established order. Most religious beliefs, especially the most widespread ones, claim there's an eternal life after death. This belief, embraced by millions around the world, may seem harmless, but that's a mistaken impression.

Let's delve into this. As I mentioned earlier, such beliefs are rooted in the fear of death. However, here I want to discuss their consequences. If there's life after death, it means our earthly existence is insignificant, devoid of value when compared to the immense reward awaiting us in the afterlife. Surely, this brief span of suffering pales in comparison to an eternity of happiness with our loved ones, provided we've earned that reward. Our known life becomes a mere fleeting moment, trivial when juxtaposed with the hereafter where we'll face God's judgment.

The implications are profound. It means that people's lives are barely worth anything, and what really matters is attaining that "hereafter" promised by religion. Once we internalize this idea, our own death becomes insignificant, especially if it's in the name of our faith.

Such beliefs illuminate many historical events. For instance, the fanatical zeal with which European Christian crusaders fought against so-called infidels to seize the Holy Land. They weren't bothered about risking their lives. If such a sacrifice earned them a place in heaven and absolved all their sins, they'd happily die for a faith they deemed as the ultimate truth.

It makes no sense to fight for a more just society if humanity's fate is to await certain death only to then enjoy eternal bliss. Such beliefs empower those who wish to maintain the status quo. People are meant to resign themselves to human suffering because that's the fate God has given them. All they can do is follow the teachings of those who claim to speak for that deity, hoping to secure eternal happiness in the next life—a happiness they couldn't find in this "vale of tears."

Rebelling against a tyrant king seen as divinely appointed is futile. Striving for fairer, more equal, and happier societies seems pointless. All these are seen as petty goals that distract from the ultimate purpose: achieving eternal life.

That's why, even in many states deemed democratic, political power promotes religion, finding it useful for its ends. The ruling elites want the status quo maintained, their privileges intact. And religion helps them achieve that. It convinces the masses to settle, not to fight for change, and to accept their bleak destiny without protest. Hence, politics has always sought, and will always seek, a closeness to religious hierarchies. Controlling people's beliefs grants immense power, and politicians aim to bolster their position by leveraging religion for their goals—to perpetuate the established social order.

In doing so, religious elites gain influence and control over their followers. More believers mean more power. Their support for the established order isn't free; it comes at a price. That's how majestic cathedrals, luxurious palaces were built, and how vast fortunes have been amassed over the centuries.

They preach the disdain for material goods, the insignificance of money and power, yet, in a glaring act of hypocrisy, they accumulate immense wealth. Political power uses religion to reinforce its privileges. And those controlling religions—religious hierarchies—gain a platform to spread their message, money, and influence. Both parties benefit from this relationship.

Religion serves many purposes in society. One relates to the identity of the group we belong to. In deeply theistic societies, it's seen as the essence of the nation, a glue binding diverse groups within a state. Being religious is equated with being a good citizen, and those who aren't religious are branded unpatriotic. When this happens, the majority faith is treated as a social good to be protected, leading to the exclusion, marginalization, or even legal persecution of those deviating from the norm.

Such behaviors pressure people to believe. In countries like the United States, despite pioneering religious freedom, there's strong social pressure against atheists or agnostics. While one can theoretically believe anything, those veering away from majority beliefs face harsh consequences. They might be ostracized by their family or hindered from ascending the social ladder. They might never aspire to a significant political role or any other powerful position requiring group endorsement. All this creates a social climate nudging people toward religion.

Identifying a religion with the state is dangerous. Separating faith from political power is undoubtedly a societal advancement worth fighting for. The public sphere must be neutral on these matters, as it's the only way to allow for dissent. It's the sole path to crafting a shared living space among diverse religious beliefs and those without them. Much has been achieved in separating church and state, but the journey remains long.

It's true that in communist regimes, religion has been persecuted, and attempts have been made, with limited success, to establish atheism in society. I see this as a mistake. Both belief and non-belief should be the result of personal decisions, and the state should not try to impose a specific philosophical conception.

Everything I've said up to this point shows us that fear drives religion: the fear of death, of the group, or of loneliness. It's not love that compels us to believe. Often, it's the desire to feel accepted. We don't want to face the consequences of making a decision that might lead us away from the paths most people follow.

It doesn't matter if we're rejected, silenced, marginalized, denied the chance to appear in the media, to hold significant political roles, or to attain any economic or social benefit. We should remain indifferent to these challenges. Truth may come at a high price, but when we grasp it, it's always worth the cost. We must be free if we wish to achieve a mindset that allows for a deeper understanding of the world.

When I talk about "dying to society," I'm not suggesting that we should isolate ourselves from others or avoid any form of social relationship. What I mean is that we shouldn't be slaves to the opinions of others; we shouldn't be overly concerned with what they think. This doesn't mean we should ignore them or believe that our thoughts are always superior.

That's not my point here. What I am saying is that the path to truth is an individual journey. To achieve this crucial goal, we must reject societal authorities and the ideas most people accept as truths. Only by following our path, in complete and utter solitude, can we truly be with others. Our relationship with them will no longer be one of subservience; instead, we can coexist harmoniously without betraying who we are.

We must die for society and be reborn in truth. We need to shun societal conventions, the prejudices ingrained in us from a young age. The path to wisdom begins when we stop parroting what others have told us and seek knowledge free from the heavy chains that others wish to place on us.